The Mirror, The Mask, and All I Ask

EL HOFFMAN

A NOTE TO READERS

As Violet once thought that her world "seemed determined to snub her" while looking into a mirror in *The Ever-Dark*, I often find myself reflecting on how I balance finding my footing with being honest. This is a collection of poetry on love, life, and grief.

PRAISE

"*The Mirror, The Mask, and All I Ask* is a hauntingly honest and beautifully crafted poetry collection that invites readers to peel back the layers of identity, loss, and longing —offering solace, strength, and a resonant voice for anyone navigating the fragile space between survival and self-discovery." – NewInBooks

CONTENT WARNING

Through an artistic lens, this collection explores themes of sexual assault, trauma, grief, and mental health. Reader discretion is advised.

"Follow the stars... because they will light the way wherever you go."
  - *The Ever-Dark*

"I Bleed Red"

Come home,
Wipe off the blue paint
I bleed red,
But you keep painting me blue

I say nothing,
I don't open my mouth
Yet you think I'm one of you,
And I'm not

I'm tired of the assumptions,
And I'm sick of being dyed
I don't bleed blue,
I just wish you could see that, too

"Contractual Obligation"

They continue asking,
but I cannot answer

"Judicial Opinion"

Lost my dollars through adversity
Dragged through trial to appease instability
Fighting unseen battles from a curse in my
    bloodstream
Black-and-white thinking in a life full of grey
Told to move on and deny my dismay
But I still have hope, no matter how hard they try

"What I Didn't Say"

Sitting here thinking
about everything that I didn't say.
Like that I love you, today

"Saltine"

I thought I didn't like humidity
Until I met true dryness
Now?
I'm a saltine cracker
Or a fish out of water
Gasping for breath

"On the Inside"

Externally happy,
But like clouds she leaks rain

"A Mistake"

By the time that you realized your mistake,
I had realized mine, too.

"*Amsterdam*"

The best city
I could never live in

"Grateful for Your Love"

Every single day of my life,
I will reiterate my gratitude for you

"No Contact"

Every day,
I grieve
those that I had to leave behind

"Meant to Be"

I feel as if
I am floating in the sea
I never knew love
Until you met me

"Starry Eyes"

Don't compliment a woman's eyes
at a dinner you paid for,
if it's not a date

"Not My Friend"

They are my friend,
while I am their afterthought

"Gaslight"

You can rewrite reality all you want,
but I remember what happened

"Tales of a Borderline Romantic"

Taking a magnifying glass to every interaction
But me desperate for clues
Is nothing new

"I See Why You Like it Here"

Walking up and down the streets,
looking at all the signs.
You posted about this once.
I could picture you standing there,
but you're not.
And I am.

"Love"

Love is like a winding road by a stream
It's the magic in a dream
Hoping it's not filled with sorrow
Waiting each day until tomorrow
Hoping everything is bright
Praying your path is winding right
Filling my eyes with the light
Smiling now and forever again
When?

"I Like You Too"

When you told me how you felt,
I got very overwhelmed.
But mostly in a good way.

"Clipped Wings"

You need to fly, you need to fly, you need to fly,
    they said to the bird with clipped wings
There is no way to get around if you don't fly.
You might die,
they said with false enthusiasm.

"Everywhere I Go"

I look for you in every room,
Every place,
Everywhere I go

"The Occupation"

You still occupy more of my mental real estate
Than I ever have of yours

"I Want You"

I want nothing more than to be in your arms
    right now,
And fall asleep beside you.
Waking up next to you
is my favorite part of the day.

"Portal Into Your Arms"

The best portal to a magical realm
is either in your arms,
in a coffee shop,
or from a coffee shop into your arms.

"Elevator"

I am stuck on you,
like when I was stuck in an elevator

"I Don't Love You"

I've been through a lot of pain,
but nothing hurts worse than
hearing the love of your life say
you aren't the love of theirs.

"A Thank You Out Into the Universe"

A thank you out into the universe
Although we haven't spoken in years,
I wanted to thank you for setting my life in motion
    that night
I wouldn't be where I am today without that
    conversation, and I'm grateful for you for that
Things are volatile now,
but I love it
I love the ever-evolving nature and every day being
    different
I'm grateful for the push in this direction, and for
    everyone I've met along the way
I love it

"First Available"

First available is for when you don't care if you get
    a booth or a table
Or inside or outside
When you're going out to eat,
Not for your choice of a place to stay

"Attraction"

Looking at an attractive woman
is like marveling at the beauty and wonder
of a snow globe

"I Miss Looking at Bananas"

I miss being at the grocery store
Standing in the aisle
Looking at bananas
Deciding if I want
Green, yellow, or brown
Organic or regular
Small or large
And how many
I didn't know the importance of freedom
Until it was gone

"What Sounds Like Apples"

Better doesn't equal good
But over a bad apple
I prefer a Granny Smith or a honey crisp
I still have the words you left written down in front
   of me
Tossed them up in the air but they're not
   coming down
I still look for yours in all that I see
But a phonetic slippage is a closer resemblance
Crumbling while stuck to the ceiling

"Near but Not Here"

Shouted your name into the abyss, as if you
    could hear
And yet I still hoped that you would be here

"A Year Too Late"

I burnt a bridge I'd been meaning to burn
But that bridge used to make my world turn
Before becoming a lesson I needed to learn
Yet some part of me will always yearn
Despite that bridge not allowing my return

"One Year Later"

Lies and negative associations
You were not who I thought you were,
Or who I hoped you'd be
The pain that you caused me
Felt never-ending
But now, I am free
I'm living life on my terms
I don't know why I ever thought
You were worth the burns
But I'm grateful for the lessons I've learned

"Around the World"

No matter what I do or where I go,
the sadness follows me everywhere

.

"Austin"

I felt like I had left something behind,
and I had.
I left a piece of my heart there.

"My Heart"

Cleave my heart in two,
For that is how it feels when I am not with you

"Saying Hello"

I waved to the pedicab driver,
but I wasn't asking for a ride

"I Mean What I Say"

But when we said forever,
I meant it

"Pros and Cons"

Anywhere that meets a lot of my criteria
does not meet all of it
As with people,
I have learned to take the good with the bad,
the black blocks with the white blocks
But nowhere, no one, and nothing is perfect
And splitting still happens

"The Divide"

Sharing similar traits doesn't mean
you think the same

"Withel"

I hope that last Christmas
was your last noel

" Herbal Tea "

We shared herbal tea,
as if we were meant to be

"A Life Worth Living"

You are like a field of flowers,
and have a life worth living

"I Think"

I loved him so much that
I think I lost a part of myself
when he left

"Just You"

Life partner excluded, I think my life
would be much more pleasant
if I never saw another that way

"Obsession"

Your love wasn't love,
it was obsession

"White Cars"

Four white cars lined up in the parking lot,
but none of them are yours

"Binoculars"

I didn't mean to carry binoculars
They just showed up in my hand one day
Head on a swivel, looking for ghosts

"Passenger"

I wish my wagon had a canopy,
a seat for me to sit in,
and speakers,
so I could live in comfort,
no matter where I go.

"Honesty"

Why be honest with him,
if he won't be honest with me?

"Night Brain"

I usually try not to send messages late at night.
I know I didn't say anything bad,
but definitely more than during daylight hours.

"Not as it Appears"

A suit and tie
doesn't mean that people
owe you their time

"Spinning"

But what was real,
and what was the story you had spun?

"The Adversary"

Bunnies hopping in the grass, along the tree line
in front of the stream
What she did not know was that the adversary was
    the one
who allowed this dream

"Pretty in Pink"

Light pink dress
and a veil with lace
If only I could
see your face

"Microwave Man"

I'm inspecting the foundation
When was the water heater last replaced?
How does the roof look?
And you're in the kitchen, staring at the microwave
Marveling at the food warmer
As if it's a religious symbol
or a historical relic,
And not just a microwave

"I Am Yours"

Like a moth to a flame,
a magnet to another,
and the gravity to the Earth,
I love you from the center of my being
More than a deep attraction to you
Everything in my heart is tied to yours
You are my everything
and I am yours

"Don't Touch My Neck"

In a moment of grief,
I can still feel your hands around my neck

"Moving"

Your voice is still in my head.
Yet despite the tears that I've shed,
and even when I'm filled with dread,
I choose to follow the path ahead.

"Too Nice"

People often assume that I'm flirting...
Because I'm too nice,
Yet people also assume I'm not flirting...
Because I'm too nice

"Black and White"

Don't speak in absolutes,
if you don't mean it absolutely

Acknowledgments

I would like to thank Sam Bolano for his work as my illustrator. I would also like to thank my readers for allowing my vision to take root in your minds.

Several of the poems included in this collection were previously published in *The Ever-Dark* and *No Other Reason*, and I'm grateful to share them with you again here.

I hope you enjoyed *The Mirror, The Mask,* and *All I Ask*. If you did, please consider leaving a review on Amazon and/or Goodreads, and if you'd like to read further, my second collection, *The Moon, The Tide, and All I Tried*, is also available.

About the Author

El Hoffman (born February 8, 2000) is an author, poet, and data expert. A lifelong writer, she debuted with *The Ever-Dark*, a literary fantasy novella. She is also the author of the romantic comedy novelette *No Other Reason* and two poetry collections: *The Mirror, The Mask, and All I Ask* and *The Moon, The Tide, and All I Tried*.

Outside of fiction, El has built a successful career implementing HubSpot for businesses and earned her Master of Science in Data Analytics from Eastern University in 2024.

When she's not writing or working, she enjoys reading ebooks, taking long walks, and hula hooping. She's also passionate about video games, cooking, exploring new restaurants, and traveling.

instagram.com/elhoffmanauthor

tiktok.com/@elhoffmanauthor

amazon.com/author/elhoffman

linkedin.com/in/elofagoodtime

bookbub.com/authors/el-hoffman

threads.com/@elhoffmanauthor

youtube.com/@elhoffmanauthor